Shaft sinkers at Thoresby Colliery, Nottinghamshire, 1924.

THE COLLIER

A. R. Griffin

Shire Publications Ltd

CONTENTS
Coal 3
Cutting the coal 5
Transporting the coal from face
  to shaft 10
Winders and haulage devices 10
Drainage and ventilation 18
Safety and rescue 21
Birth of a mining community 24
Life in a mining community 27
Postscript 31

Copyright © 1982 by A. R. Griffin. First published 1982; reprinted 1986, 1990. Shire Album 82. ISBN 0 85263 590 7.
All rights reserved. No part of this publication may be reproduced or transmitted in any form or by any means, electronic or mechanical, including photocopy, recording, or any information storage and retrieval system, without permission in writing from the publishers, Shire Publications Ltd, Cromwell House, Church Street, Princes Risborough, Aylesbury, Bucks, HP17 9AJ, UK.

Set in 10 on 9 point Times roman and printed in Great Britain by C. I. Thomas & Sons (Haverfordwest) Ltd, Press Buildings, Merlins Bridge, Haverfordwest.

ACKNOWLEDGEMENTS
The photographs are from the comprehensive collection at the National Mining Museum, Lound Hall. The author's thanks for permission to reproduce illustrations are due to the following: C. Lowde, page 1; R. H. Childs, Estates and Mineral Director, Clay Cross Company Ltd, pages 2, 8, 15 (bottom), 16 (bottom), 42; Coalville Technical College, page 12 (bottom); the late Fred Smith, page 13; E. Williamson, pages 16 (top), 20 (bottom); D. E. Jenkins, page 20 (top); and I. K. Griffin for the line drawings.

COVER: 'The Collier', an illustration from 'The Costume of Yorkshire' by George Walker, published in the mid nineteenth century.

A postcard of c 1900 showing one collier breaking down the coal with a pick and another setting a prop. Note the safety lamps and, in the background, a small wagon (a 'tub' or 'tram') for conveying the coal out of the mine. This is one of a series of pictures issued on postcards by the Clay Cross Company, Derbyshire, to advertise their coal.

Colliers working a shallow pit during the 1926 strike using 'home-made' hand winding gear. This woodland scene is reminiscent of medieval coalmining.

COAL

The *Concise Oxford Dictionary* defines coal as: 'hard opaque black or blackish mineral of carbonised vegetable matter found in seams or strata below earth's surface and used as fuel and in manufacture of gas, tar, etc.'

Coal seams were formed many millions of years ago from the rotting vegetation of tropical forests, just as peat is being formed today in the Ganges delta. Layers of sediment deposited on top of this composted material gradually compressed it until it became coal. Intermediate between peat and the bituminous coal which we use for domestic and industrial heating is lignite *(brown coal)*, which is rare in Britain but fairly abundant in Germany. Most bituminous coals are suitable for raising steam and in Britain the largest consumer is the electricity generating industry, which used 80.7 million tonnes of the total of 103.5 million tonnes produced in 1988-9 for driving its steam turbines. A few areas (especially Durham) produce coal which is particularly good for the manufacture of metallurgical coke; whilst in South Wales is found anthracite, a type of coal which burns almost smokelessly and which is now in great demand for central heating in smokeless zones.

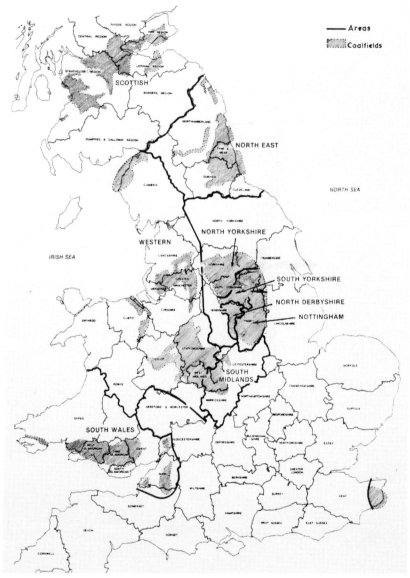

British Coal Corporation Areas as they were in 1987.

STATISTICAL SUMMARY FOR 1988-9

British Coal Areas and Groups	number of mines	saleable output (thousands of tonnes)	year end manpower (thousands)
North Yorkshire	14	16,141	12.5
South Yorkshire	18	13,289	13.1
Nottinghamshire	16	17,184	15.2
Central	8	10,876	10.2
Scottish	2	1,927	2.4
North East	7	10,348	11.1
North West	11	9,809	9.6
South Wales	9	5,018	6.9
Kent	1	444	0.7
Total	86	85,035	81.7

This table of the output and manpower figures for 1988-9 is for British Coal's deep mines only. In addition, opencast quarries produce 16.8 million tonnes and private mines 1.7 million tonnes.

CUTTING THE COAL

Movements in the earth's crust have caused coal seams to be inclined rather than horizontal and this, together with the effects of volcanic, glacial and climatic action, has exposed the edges of most seams. The exposed edge of a seam is called the outcrop or basset edge. The earliest coal workings were on these outcrops, the coal being dug where it was exposed. Evidence of shallow coal was often found on riverbanks.

The combustible properties of coal were probably first recognised in ancient China. In Britain it has certainly been used since Roman times, if not before. The earliest written records of coalmining date from the later medieval period when coal was dug from the soil by peasants, who regarded it rather as a specialist form of agriculture.

Once the surface deposits were gone, there were two ways of proceeding. On hills it was usual to drive tunnels (or *drifts*) into the seam for a short distance. On flat ground shallow pits rather like wells were sunk down to the seam. The coal was then dug from around the pit bottom by sharp-pointed picks until the sides of the pit were in danger of collapsing, when the pit was abandoned and another dug nearby. Seen in section, such a pit is shaped like a bell, so we call them *bell pits*. At depths of more than about 20 feet (6 m), labour was economised by heading out into the seam, and it was found that connecting two or more shafts together allowed air to flow, so enabling them to honeycomb the seam with a network of tunnels from which the coal had been *got*, separated by pillars of coal left to support the roof. This stall (or *bord*) and pillar system was once universal, and a few examples are still found in Northumberland and Durham today.

In this system the bord was usually worked by one man on his own. First, he undercut the coal to a depth of several feet; then he cut nicks up each side of the bord, so enabling him to break the coal down by driving wedges into it with a hammer. The large lumps were then broken up with a pick.

The alternative system, which developed first in Shropshire in the seventeenth cen-

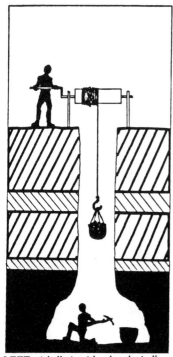

LEFT: *A bell pit with a hand windlass, showing how coal was wound manually from a shallow seam. This device was in use from the middle ages, and some small mines have used them in the twentieth century. Bell pits are so called because, seen in section, they have the shape of bells.*
RIGHT: *A modern open-cast site where eighteenth-century bord and pillar has been exposed. Some roadways are cut to a lower level than others to make height for the ponies.*

tury, and of which there have been many variants, enabled a number of men to work co-operatively on one long coal face. From the middle of the nineteenth until well into the twentieth century the chief variant was the system known as *longwall tub-stall*, and this is still practised today at a few small privately owned mines. First, a main roadway was driven out from the pit bottom some distance into the seam, leaving an unworked pillar of coal around the shaft to give it support. On each side of this roadway, subsidiary main roads were driven at intervals and working faces were opened out on either side of these. Whereas with early coal mines (say pre-1850) all roadways were commonly driven entirely in coal, so that the height of a roadway was the same as the thickness of the seam (which could be 3 feet, 0.9 m, or less) in later practice most roadways were made high enough to allow men and ponies to travel along them comfortably. However, the actual coal faces were (and are) still as high as the seam is thick, typically between 1 and 2 metres (40-80 inches). The roadways were supported by substantial *puncheons* of wood set vertically, usually with horizontal wooden bars over them pressed up to the roof.

With all variants of longwall the first process at the coal face was to undercut the coal using a sharp-pointed pick. This work (called *holing* or *curving*) was arduous. Having cut along the floor of the seam for 8 or 10 inches (200-250 mm), the *holer* set *catch props* under the cut to prevent the coal falling whilst he was cutting. He would then extend his cut to 4 feet (1.2 m) or so under the seam, necessitating putting his head and trunk at risk. On a coal face 100 metres (328 feet) long, two men would do all the cutting.

The cut completed, the *getters* knocked

A longwall face in thick seam workings, probably in Warwickshire, taken about 1910 by the Reverend F. W. Cobb. Note the two men undercutting the seam protected by props. The man at the right is making a hole for gunpowder.

out the catch props with a hammer, allowing the weight of the coal to bear down. Then the coal was *got* by hammering wedges into the face and levering lumps down with the pick or (in later practice) a long iron crowbar called a *ringer*. Before the industrial revolution, iron was so expensive that hammers, wedges and shovels were made from wood. Iron tools (other than pick heads) only became common from about 1780. From about 1830, gunpowder came into use at the coal face to help to break the coal down. Holes were made in the coal by a chisel-pointed round iron bar called a *jumper* (later by drills) and into each hole a quantity of gunpowder was poured. Some kind of fuse (often a straw filled with gunpowder) was put into the hole, and the mouth of the hole stemmed with clay. Then the shotfirer lit the fuse and moved away as quickly as possible.

For the house coal market, large coal was wanted, so the use of gunpowder was restricted and in many cases forbidden.

Having broken the coal into lumps of suitable size, the men loaded it into baskets (before about 1845) or into small wagons called *tubs* or *trams*, to be transported out of the mine.

The first coal face operation to be mechanised was the undercutting of the coal. The earliest coal-cutting machines, dating from the 1850s, were unsuccessful because of the lack of a suitable power source. In the 1870s compressed air became available, followed in the 1890s by electricity, but there were few cutting machines in use before the twentieth century. Indeed, even in 1913 only 8.5 per cent of British coal was mechanically cut; this rose to 31 per cent in 1930 and 73.9 per cent in 1946.

These machines were of three types. One had a disc with picks slotted around its

A typical collier of around 1900, as shown on another of the Clay Cross postcards.

periphery, which was made to rotate like a circular saw along the floor of the seam whilst the machine travelled along the face. Another had a rotating round iron bar set with picks; and the third had a chain laced with picks travelling around an iron jib. All three took a cut of about 4 inches (100 mm) from the floor of the seam thus producing much less small coal than the hand holer, who necessarily took a much bigger cut because he had to get his body into it to reach far enough back.

These machines still left the getting and filling operations to be done by hand. However, during the Second World War a new breed of *power loading* machines began to evolve. These machines cut the whole section of coal to be worked and loaded it mechanically on to a moving iron conveyor belt (the armoured face conveyor or *panzer*) running along the face. By the 1970s, some 97 or 98 per cent of all coal produced in Britain was power loaded.

ABOVE: *An early coal-cutting machine in the yard seam at Walsall Wood Colliery, West Midlands. This was a 'Peake-English' bar machine used at Pelsall Colliery before 1900, and in use at Walsall Wood until about 1916. It was more usual to undercut the coal than to overcut it as in this example. In the foreground is an acetylene lamp, not safe to use where explosive gas was likely to be present.*
BELOW: *A modern coal face at Warsop Colliery, Derbyshire. In the distance is seen a 'trepanner' (a machine which cuts coal by boring like a giant augur). The coal drops on to a moving steel 'panzer' conveyor and the face is supported by self advancing hydraulic chocks.*

This illustration of a girl wearing a dog-belt pulling a tram is based upon the illustration in the Children's Employment Commission Report of 1842.

TRANSPORTING THE COAL FROM FACE TO SHAFT

With early drift (i.e. tunnel) mines, coal was loaded into baskets or boxes, which were either carried or pulled along the floor. A small drift mine in Shropshire (the Foxhills *footridge*) was still using a wooden box, pulled manually by a length of rope, in this way as recently as 1915. There is some evidence of the early use of wheelbarrows in coal mines too.

Baskets (or *corves*) made from plaited hazel wands were used in most coalfields until well into the nineteenth century. In the Scottish *stair pits,* women carried the coal in baskets on their backs along the underground tunnels and up ladders to the pit top as recently as the 1840s. In the East Midlands, donkeys driven by young boys were employed at this period to draw the corves to the main roadways, where they were loaded on to wheeled carriages (called *trams*) which ran on rails to the pit bottom. The *ass-lad* had to control the movement of the corf with a leather *dog-belt* which he wore round his hips and which was attached to the corf by a chain and hook. Where the roadways were too low for donkeys, children drew the corves (or in some cases wheeled trams) with the dog-belt, either on hands and knees or bent double. For example, this was fairly common in West Yorkshire, where both boys and girls were employed. Sometimes a rope harness, called a *guss,* was used instead of a dog-belt, and this device was still used at a few Somerset collieries in 1947.

In Northumberland and Durham the corves were drawn on sledges to the main roadways by boys, then loaded by a crane on to long wheeled carriages *(rollies),* running on rails.

Rails, first introduced underground about 1760, were laid only on the main roads until after the change in shaft technology which took place about 1840 and which is described in the next chapter.

WINDERS AND HAULAGE DEVICES

The hand windlass was the earliest winding device, and some small pits have used it in the twentieth century. In particular, miners working outcrop coal during the great strikes of 1893, 1912, 1921 and 1926 employed methods and equipment, including simple windlasses sometimes made from bicycle wheels and mangles, virtually identical to those of their forebears of generations ago.

There have been for centuries considerable variations in the depths of shafts. Today, there are a few more than 1,000 metres (3,280 feet) deep, but even in the early seventeenth century 50 to 60 metres (160-200 feet) was not an unusual depth on Tyneside, where the most rapid development of coalmining took place because of the availability of sea transport to London, where much coal was consumed. To cope with the increasing depth, a horse-drawn windlass (the *cog-and-rung gin*) came into use, followed towards the end of the seventeenth century by the *whim gin*. Here, a rope wound round a horizontal drum passes over a pulley wheel and down the shaft. Attached to the drum is a horizontal wooden bar, and a horse is harnessed to this and is then made to walk round in a circle. As it does so, the rope with a corf attached is first lowered into the shaft to be filled and then raised to the surface. Because the rope is of fixed length, the horse always walks in the same direction.

During the eighteenth century, deeper and deeper shafts became common in the more developed areas, and whim gins with two, four and even eight horses were used. But, towards the century's close, the steam engines of Newcomen and Watt (which were originally designed to pump water out of mines) were adapted to rotary motion

RIGHT: *The cog-and-rung gin was an adaptation of the windlass for horse traction in the early seventeenth century for use at the deeper mines that were then developing. This device was later displaced by the whim gin.*
BELOW: *This replica of a whim gin is now at the Chatterley Whitfield Mining Museum, Tunstall, Staffordshire.*

ABOVE: *An atmospheric winding engine at Teversal, Nottinghamshire, c 1865. On the left is the banksman and winding engineman, Hezekiah Cheetham, and on the right Mr Hobson, the colliery enginewright. This pit used a flat winding rope with chain attachments, and the noise this made gave it its name 'Nibland', short for 'Nibble-and-clink'.*
BELOW: *Heather Colliery, Leicestershire, c 1860, a late example of a shaft where corves were still in use for raising coal.*

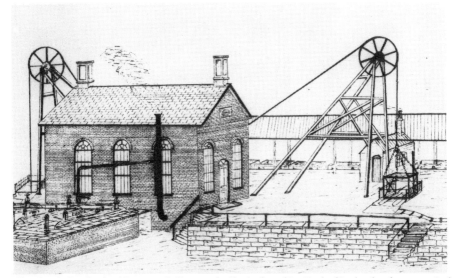

This detail of a sketch of Langton Colliery on the Nottinghamshire-Derbyshire border shows a typical cage of the 1840s. The winding engine was of the new horizontal twin-cylinder pattern with a rope drum mounted on the far-side wall of the engine house drawing coal from two shafts.

and used as winding engines. Both were similar in appearance. A large wooden beam, pivoted at its centre, was made to rock up and down by a piston to which one end was attached by a chain or rod. For pumping, the other end of the beam was attached by a chain to pump rods operating in pipes *(pump trees)* in the shaft. For winding, rotary motion was achieved by a crank and flywheel or some similar device. Before the 1840s, most of these winders were of the Newcomen type (with open-top cylinders) and not of the Watt type (with separate condensers) as the older history books say. These early engines employed steam at low pressures, 8 to 15 hp (6-11 kW) being common even in the early 1840s, but between 1840 and 1860 high-pressure engines became necessary as the average size of the undertaking grew. Some had vertical cylinders, but increasingly the bicylindrical horizontal arrangement predominated. There are still about twenty of these in use, but all will soon be replaced by electrically driven engines. The fine engines at Sherwood Colliery, Mansfield, will be among the last to be replaced.

The cage held steady in the shaft by guide rods (or rails) was invented by T. Y. Hall in 1835 and the new system (the *cage tub and guide rod system*) of haulage came into general use between 1840 and 1860. Formerly, coal had been loaded into corves at the coal face, the corves were pulled and pushed by boys or donkeys on sledges to the main road, then lifted on to trams or rolleys to run on rails to the pit bottom, then lifted off and secured by a hook to the hempen winding rope which swung freely in the shaft. Now, the coal was loaded directly into wheeled tubs (rectangular wooden boxes) at the coal face and brought on rails all the way to the pit bottom; the tubs were pushed on to the cage (which was also fitted with rails); the cage ascended the shaft, held steady by guide rods or rails, and at the pit top the tubs were pushed on to yet more rails to be hauled to the screening plant, where men and boys (or, in Lancashire, women, the so-called *pit-brow lassies*) removed the dirt and sorted the coal into various qualities. This new system quadrupled shaft capacity, some shafts raising 1,000 tonnes or more in an eight or

A winding engineman at Walsall Wood Colliery, West Midlands, in the early years of the twentieth century. This is a typical winding engine house of the period. The engine was built by Thornewill and Warham, Burton upon Trent, about 1880 and its two cylinders were 28 inches by 6 feet (0.7 by 1.8 metres), using steam at 100 pounds per square inch. The rope drum (seen on the left of the picture) was of the spiral-cylindrical type. This engine was replaced by an electric winder in 1954. There are now very few steam winding engines in operation.

ten hour shift. Also, for the men, riding the shaft in a cage was a vast improvement on the previous method of clinging to a loop in a rope.

The availability of rails all the way from face to wagon encouraged the introduction of boilers and stationary steam engines underground to replace boys and ponies, although because of the danger of explosions this practice was soon succeeded by either taking the steam underground in pipes from surface boilers or having a haulage engine on the surface driving a haulage rope over a pulley wheel at the pit top, down the shaft, then round further pulley wheels underground. The tubs were attached by clips to the rope.

In the late nineteenth and early twentieth centuries compressed air sometimes took the place of steam in haulage engines; but both have since given way to diesel and electricity.

At some collieries large wagons called *mine cars*, hauled by diesel (or, more rarely, electric battery driven) locomotives, bring the coal to the shaft. At others, transport is by a series of conveyor belts made from flameproof PVC.

At the coal face, rubber conveyor belts to take the coal to the main *gate* (i.e. roadway) were gradually introduced during the inter-war period. These had to be dismantled and re-erected manually each day as the coal face advanced. Now, the steel *panzer* conveyor is connected to the hydraulically operated chocks which support the face, providing what is virtually a canopy of steel. As the face advances, the chocks and conveyor are moved forward by hydraulic power operated by keys attached either to individual chocks or to batches of chocks. Further, in most cases the power loading machines are mounted on the conveyor, so these move over too in the same operation.

Support systems have improved on haulage roads as well as at the coal face. In place of wooden *puncheons*, steel arched girders, with corrugated steel linings, are almost universally used, and a main underground roadway looks very much like the London 'tube'.

Modern haulage systems have not completely eliminated the pit pony because

ABOVE: *This picture, taken by the Reverend F. W. Cobb about 1910, shows a boy leading a pony underground at Brinsley Colliery, Nottinghamshire. It was obviously posed for the photographer: normally, the pony would be urged on to go as fast as conditions allowed.*
BELOW: *Another of the Clay Cross postcards showing a busy pit-bottom scene in the early years of the twentieth century. Note the full tubs being pushed on to the cage, and the empty ones being pushed 'inbye' (i.e. towards the coal face).*

ABOVE: *A group of miners at the pit top at Alfreton Colliery, Derbyshire, in 1926. Those with clean faces on the left-hand side are afternoon-shift men about to descend, whilst those on the right-hand side with dirty faces are the day-shift men who have just stepped off the cage at the end of their shift.*

BELOW: *Making the roof safe at Clay Cross, about 1900.*

Steel arches support this roadway in a modern mine (Shirebrook, Derbyshire). Compare this with the previous photograph.

there are still a few collieries in Durham and South Wales which use them for transporting materials. Shetland ponies were first introduced underground in Durham and Northumberland in the mid eighteenth century, but at collieries working thick seams, Welsh and Dales cobs and even Shire horses have been used. They were always geldings. By 1912, there were over 70,000 ponies underground, and even in 1951 there were still 15,858. Except at a few drift mines, ponies were stabled underground and rarely saw the light of day. Once accustomed to life underground, where they were warm, well fed, well groomed and generally made much of by the men, they seemed happy enough. On the rare occasions when they were wound out to grass (not an easy operation) they were understandably frisky.

An underground ventilation furnace at Walsall Wood, West Midlands, the last colliery to use this form of ventilation.

DRAINAGE AND VENTILATION

Water was the early mine owner's greatest problem. Where his workings were on hilly ground, he could drive a water level or *sough* to daylight. In other cases, his water level discharged water into a well (a *sump*) from which it could be wound out by bucket or pumped out by a primitive horse-driven *gin* like the rag and chain pump or chain of buckets. Not until the introduction of the Newcomen engine in the early eighteenth century was there a reliable device for draining mines at any great depth. At Peggs Green in Leicestershire, a beam engine installed in 1805 and typical of the period discharged 750 gallons (3,410 litres) of water a minute.

Some collieries are far wetter than others, but a typical deep mine of the 1980s will discharge about 200,000 gallons (900,000 litres) a month, although some discharge over a million gallons (4.5 million litres) a month, using electrically driven pumps, mostly of the submersible type, which have replaced steam engines. The only Newcomen pumping engine still *in situ* and in working order is at Elsecar Colliery in South Yorkshire. It can be viewed on request. Another steam-driven pump of 1900 vintage can be seen at the National Mining Museum, Lound Hall.

A great deal of water is encountered in sinking shafts; and in the twentieth century freezing the ground before commencing to sink has been increasingly practised. Shafts, once sunk, are kept dry by lining them with *tubbing*. In the eighteenth century, this was made like a wooden cask or tub (hence the name) but iron came into use in the nineteenth century.

In the South Wales valleys, where pit tips are often on hillsides, water has at times made the tips unstable, as at Aberfan, where 144 men, women and children were killed by a slippage of colliery spoil in 1966. Special care is taken to ensure that this can never be repeated.

18

In early mining practice, ventilation was achieved by linking together two shafts and allowing air to flow between them by natural convection. The flow of air could be improved by suspending a fire basket (like a nightwatchman's brazier) in one of the shafts. The warm air rising in the *upcast* shaft caused a partial vacuum in the workings and cold air flowed down the *downcast* shaft to maintain the balance of the air pressure. A few collieries used fire baskets in the seventeenth century, but the practice did not become widespread until the eighteenth.

In 1787 an underground ventilation furnace was built at Wallsend Colliery near Newcastle and owners of other deep mines soon adopted the practice. Whilst a large furnace undoubtedly improved ventilation, there was always the danger of explosion from gas-laden air passing over the fire. This danger was eliminated in the early nineteenth century by isolating the foul air from the fire by means of a dumb drift (see sketch). From the mid nineteenth century mechanical fans began to replace furnaces but the last of these (at Walsall Wood Colliery, West Midlands) did not go out of use until 1950.

To guide the air round the workings it is necessary to have a system of doors and stoppings. Nowadays the doors are spring-loaded, but up to the mid nineteenth century boys called *trappers* were employed to close the doors after ponies had passed.

The main mine gases are *chokedamp* (or *blackdamp*) and *firedamp*. As its colloquial name indicates, chokedamp makes breathing difficult, and, in high concentration, impossible. Firedamp is not poisonous but when mixed with air in the proportions of between five and fifteen parts per hundred, it is explosive. Efficient ventilation dilutes these gases at the same time as it provides reasonably clean air to breathe. However, in the early nineteenth century ventilation of the deep, gassy mines of Northumberland, Durham and Cumberland was not efficient, and there were many explosions resulting from the use of candles. Carlyle Spedding of Whitehaven invented a device, the flint and steel mill, which produced a stream of sparks. This was a little safer than a candle, but it was not until Sir Humphry Davy's invention of his safety lamp in 1815 that miners were provided with a safe light. Here, the flame of an oil lamp is completely surrounded by gauze, which distributes the heat of the flame over its surface area so that at no one point is the gauze hot enough to fire an explosive mixture. Modern safety lamps, still based on Davy's principle, are used for gas testing. Illumination is now provided by electricity. Besides the fixed electric lights on the roadways, every miner has a cap lamp which gives a brilliant light.

How the dumb drift was used to isolate ventilation furnaces from the foul air of the mine.

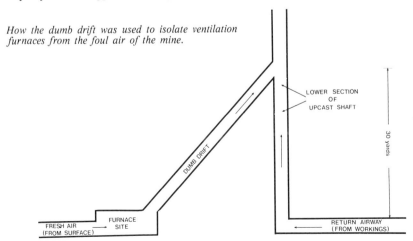

LONGITUDINAL SECTION THROUGH FURNACE

ABOVE: *The peculiar geography of the South Wales coalfield, where so many pits were squeezed into narrow valleys between high hills, has produced its own hazard of earth movement. This picture, taken about 1934, shows the catastrophic effect of earth movement on New Tredegar Colliery.*

BELOW: *The winding engine house fire at Cotes Park Colliery, Nottinghamshire, 1909. Every colliery has to have two or more shafts, so the men underground were able to come out of the pit by another shaft. Had all else failed, the Rescue Brigade's emergency winder could have been used.*

A typical colliery rescue team wearing breathing apparatus, about 1914.

SAFETY AND RESCUE

Whatever precautions are taken, some accidents are bound to occur, so first aid rooms and rescue services are provided. Such facilities have improved immeasurably over the last half century. Fire is an ever present hazard with any industrial building where there are combustible materials like oil and grease. At a colliery, such a surface fire can cause immense damage in a very short time, so every pit has its volunteer fire-fighting teams, many of which attain a very high level of efficiency. If a winding engine house or headgear is damaged by fire (or by anything else) clearly the men underground are endangered, so the Central Rescue Stations, which are to be found in all coalfields, have emergency portable winding apparatus which can, if necessary, be used to bring the men out of the mine. This is a very rare occurrence.

Fire underground, usually resulting from spontaneous combustion of small coal left in the *goaf* (i.e. the area from which the coal has been extracted) is unfortunately far from rare in some seams like the Barnsley bed of Yorkshire. This is one of the hazards which the volunteer rescue workers at the collieries and the full-time Rescue Brigadesmen from the Central Rescue Station are especially trained to tackle. The general principle is to seal off the area in which the heating is taking place, so as to rob it of oxygen.

Professor Faraday asserted after the Haswell explosion of 1844 that most, if not all, the ninety-five men and boys who lost their lives were killed by the carbon monoxide given off by burning coal dust, and not by the explosion itself. After an explosion or an underground fire, the rescue men take canaries underground with them because small birds react quickly to carbon monoxide and therefore give early warning of its presence. The illustration on page 22 shows a canary used following the most serious mine disaster in Britain, which killed 440 men and boys at Senghenydd, Mid

Glamorgan, in 1913.

For the immediate protection of the workmen, everyone going underground is nowadays compelled to carry a self-rescuer, which protects against carbon monoxide poisoning, enabling its wearer to travel to a place of safety. Other items of safety equipment which are compulsory today include the helmet and approved safety boots. When safety helmets were first introduced in the 1930s some colliery companies like Powell Duffryn of South Wales went to great lengths to persuade miners to wear them, but they met with considerable resistance, especially from some of the older colliers.

The efficient ventilation system of today and the precautions taken to prevent fire and sparking from electrical apparatus make ignitions of inflammable gas extremely rare. Where such ignitions did take place in the past, the main force of any resulting explosion was provided by coal dust rather than the gas itself.

Cutting machines today are fitted with water sprays to keep down the dust for general health reasons. Also, limestone dust is mixed liberally with coal dust on the roadways so as to render it inert and stone dust or water barriers are provided at intervals along the roadways. These various precautions have virtually eliminated any future risk of large-scale mining disasters, with which the industry used to be plagued.

A disaster at Universal Pit, Senghenydd, Mid Glamorgan, took place on 14th October 1913 and 440 men and boys were killed. It was a firedamp explosion where the ignition was caused by sparking either from electric signalling apparatus or from falling rocks. As in all such disasters, however, most of the men died from carbon monoxide poisoning rather than from the direct effect of the explosion. The photograph shows the canary taken underground by rescue men to test for carbon monoxide.

ABOVE: *The Chesterfield Mines Rescue Brigade in 1924. These early permanent rescue stations were modelled on the fire service.*
BELOW: *The volunteer colliery fire brigade at the Powell Duffryn Colliery's Elliott Colliery in the 1930s.*

Sinking a shaft of a coal mine. Here we see one of the temporary sinking head frames with a 'hoppit' or 'kibble' poised over the shaft. The men descended in this and then used it for loading out the sinking dirt.

BIRTH OF A MINING COMMUNITY

In its early days coalmining was a very small-scale activity; and miners were part of the general rural community. A growth in the demand for coal in the sixteenth and seventeenth centuries, which was felt most strongly in Northumberland and Durham, encouraged the growth of colliery villages where pitmen were seen as almost a race apart. With the further increase in demand in the industrial revolution period, the industry grew at a much faster pace. The growth of a network of turnpike roads and canals, followed from 1830 by railways, widened the market area for collieries whose growth had previously been stunted by inadequate transport facilities.

Also, improved techniques for proving deep coal measures and for mining the coal once the seams had been proved enabled the industry to expand into areas away from the old centres of production. New mining communities springing up in *greenfield* sites marked the development of coalmining in the second half of the nineteenth century and the early twentieth, especially in Durham, North Nottinghamshire, South Yorkshire and South Wales.

First, deep boreholes were put down to prove the coal. Then shafts were sunk, usually by specialist shaft sinkers, who were very much like the navvies who built the canals and railways. These men were housed in temporary hutments. Some brought womenfolk with them, but there was usually a preponderance of males and they tended to be boisterous, hard working, hard drinking, and with a reputation for gambling and loose behaviour. After the sinking and development work was complete, many of the sinkers moved on, but usually a few stayed, forming part of the

ABOVE: *Three of the sinkers standing over a shaft in which the brick lining has apparently just been completed. Note the tarpaulins and the traditional sinkers' headgear. Shaft sinking is a very wet job, and six-hour shifts are usual for this work.*
BELOW: *The sinkers' huts, typical of their kind.*

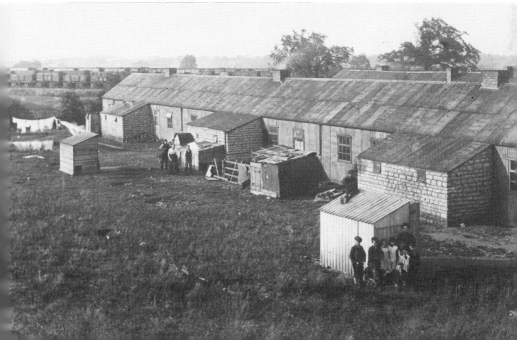

ABOVE: *Colliers' houses under construction. Note the use of the temporary railway line for carrying building materials.*
BELOW: *The public house, shops and (at the top of the hill) the manager's house are completed, but the road is still unmade. Note the railway wagon in the middle of the main street, between the pub and the shops.*

permanent labour force of the colliery. To attract labour, the colliery owners provided houses, shops, schools, churches and other community facilities, although some speculative builders would also often add to the building activity of the new village. With the growth of local government, much of the responsibility for the community facilities passed to it from colliery owners although even today in many colliery villages the social life still revolves round miners' welfare institutes with their sports and other activities.

Shirebrook in Derbyshire is a typical late nineteenth-century colliery village built on a greenfield site, and the accompanying pictures are taken from a comprehensive collection made available to the author by Mr E. Tomlinson.

LIFE IN A MINING COMMUNITY

There are some coalmining areas where mines have mainly been quite small and set out in a rural environment and where, in consequence, many colliers' houses have been scattered amongst those of other country dwellers: farm labourers, blacksmiths, carters, smallholders and so on. Again, some coal mines have been sunk in or near existing urban areas and have drawn much of their labour from the town. In both cases colliers and their families, having lived cheek by jowl with people dependent on a wide variety of occupations, have never formed separate communities.

However, as in the case of Shirebrook, there are many places where mining folk have always lived in colliery villages where almost everyone is dependent on the pit for a living, either directly or indirectly. With improvements in public transport and, more recently, the widespread ownership of motor cars, the former isolation of mining villages has been much reduced but it has been by no means eliminated. Today perhaps the isolation is partly psychological: people living in a coalmining environment sometimes feel themselves to be in some way different from others. They belong, as it were, to a fraternity of mining folk.

Every coalfield still has examples of the

Pit-brow lassies on the screening plant at the Atherton Collieries, Greater Manchester, early twentieth century.

old colliers' rows of terraced houses clustered around the pits, although most of those which survive have been improved. For example, very few black-leaded hearths, with a boiler on one side of the fire and an oven on the other, remain. And no collier nowadays has his bath (or *stripwash*) in a tin bath on the hearth or at the kitchen sink, as most of them did before pithead baths were introduced between about 1925 and 1945. Indeed, amongst the older colliers, there were a few who refused to use the baths and who continued to travel home in their pit dirt until they died or retired.

But whilst colliers' rows do still exist, most miners live in more modern properties provided either by the colliery companies in the inter-war period, or by a subsidiary of the NCB since 1947, or by a local authority or private builder. But the newer miners' housing estates, with their semi-detached houses and short terraces, do not seem to generate the same warmth of community feeling as the traditional colliery village with its cluster of long rows. There is more privacy now but less sharing. The increased prosperity has something to do with this: a shared adversity undoubtedly draws people together. Television is also partly to blame. Watching television has largely taken the place, for example, of the games traditionally played by children in the spaces between the long rows.

In the older colliery villages, most colliers had allotments and since the pits rarely worked full-time during the summer months before 1939 there was plenty of time for growing the family's vegetables.

Many men also kept poultry and in some places pigsties were also provided on the allotments. Again, every mining village had pigeon fanciers (and still has, though not as many as formerly). Other sports which have always had considerable support in colliery communities include fishing and

A collier having a 'bath' in front of the fire about 1910. Pithead baths have proved a godsend to miners' wives.

ABOVE: *A typical colliers' row in South Wales.*
BELOW: *In Roman Britain coal was mined from surface deposits. Here we see colliers, during the mining dispute in 1893, doing the same thing.*

ABOVE: *Policemen guarding Sutton Colliery, Nottinghamshire, during a strike in 1896. The company directors are in the foreground.*
BELOW: *Most miners' lodges (trade union branches) have colourful banners. This is a particularly interesting one, from Chopwell Colliery, Durham, often referred to as 'little Moscow'. It bears a portrait of Karl Marx, as well as one of Keir Hardie, and the symbols of both the Labour Party and the Communist Party.*

whippet racing.

Many colliery companies encouraged group activities like football, cricket, brass bands and the St John Ambulance Brigade and Red Cross, besides giving financial and other help to various church organisations. Some also provided welfare institutes, where various indoor and outdoor games were played, and where there were often small libraries or reading rooms. Since the establishment of the Miners' Welfare Commission in the 1920s (now replaced by the Coal Industry Social Welfare Organisation) such provision has grown appreciably, although there is, perhaps, rather less emphasis on cultural activities, and rather more on the purely social (including the ubiquitous bingo) than there used to be.

POSTSCRIPT

Miners' district unions were traditionally powerful, but they were greatly weakened by their defeat at the end of the seven-month long dispute of 1926, and they remained so until the demand for coal improved with the rearmament boom beginning in 1937. For years they had demanded nationalisation of the mines, and this was achieved on 1st January 1947, by which time the district associations had merged into the National Union of Mineworkers (NUM).

The National Coal Board inherited in 1947 980 collieries employing 704,000 men and producing 180 million tonnes of coal a year. In 1984, there were only 170 collieries employing 181,000 men and producing 90 million tonnes of deep-mined coal. This contraction was necessitated partly by exhaustion of reserves in the older mining districts and partly by the need to concentrate on the more economically viable mines to meet the competition from fuel oil, which was very cheap in the 1960s. The rundown could not have taken place so smoothly had it not been for the co-operation of the unions.

Clearly, Britain's (and the world's) coal reserves will last much longer than oil and natural gas, and there seems little doubt that coal will still be needed as a fuel well into the twenty-first century and probably beyond. It is also the raw material for dozens of by-products which are virtually indispensable in modern society. So a great deal of coal will be required for as far ahead as anyone can see.

Going home at the end of a nine-hour shift of backbreaking toil, Clay Cross, c 1900.

PLACES TO VISIT

Beamish: North of England Open Air Museum, Beamish Hall, Stanley, County Durham. Telephone: Stanley (0207) 231811.
Big Pit Mining Museum, Big Pit, Blaenavon, Gwent NP4 9XP. Telephone: Blaenavon (0495) 790311.
Black Country Museum, Tipton Road, Dudley, West Midlands DY1 4SQ. Telephone: 021-557 9643 or 9644.
Blists Hill Open Air Museum, Legges Way, Madeley, Telford, Shropshire. Telephone: Telford (0952) 586063.
Calderdale Industrial Museum, Central Works, Halifax. Telephone: Halifax (0422) 59031.
Chatterley Whitfield Mining Museum, Chatterley Whitfield Colliery, Tunstall, Stoke-on-Trent ST6 8UN. Telephone: Stoke-on-Trent (0782) 813337.
Nantgarw Colliery, near Caerphilly. Tour of surface of mine, by bus from Cardiff. Enquiries to Wales Tourist Board Information Centre. Telephone: Cardiff (0222) 27281.
Red Rose Live Steam Group, Astley Green Colliery, Astley, Tyldesley, Greater Manchester.
Salford Museum of Mining, Buile Hill Park, Eccles Old Road, Salford M6 8GL. Telephone: 061-736 1832.
Scottish Mining Museum, Prestongrange, East Lothian EH32 9RX. (Also the Lady Victoria Colliery, Midlothian.)
Tom Leonard Mining Museum, Skinningrove (off A174), Saltburn-by-the-Sea, Cleveland.
Washington 'F' Pit Museum, Albany Way, Washington, Tyne and Wear. Telephone: Washington (091) 4167640.
Welsh Industrial and Maritime Museum, Bute Street, Cardiff. Telephone: Cardiff (0222) 481919.
Welsh Miners' Museum, Afan Argoed Country Park, Cynonville, Port Talbot, West Glamorgan. Telephone: Cymmer (0639) 850564.
Wigan Pier Heritage Centre, Wigan Pier, Wigan WN3 4EU. Telephone: Wigan (0942) 323666.
Yorkshire Mining Museum, Caphouse Colliery, New Road, Overton, near Wakefield WF4 4RF. Telephone: Wakekfield (0924) 848806.

FURTHER READING

Atkinson, F. *The Great Northern Coalfield*. Newcastle, 1966.
Down, C. G. and Warrington, A. J. *The History of the Somerset Coalfield*. Newton Abbot, 1972.
Duckham, B. F. *The Scottish Coal Industry, 1705-1815*. Newton Abbot, 1970.
Galloway, R. L. *Annals of Coal Mining and the Coal Trade*. 2 volumes, 1898, 1904. Reprinted Newton Abbot, 1970.
Griffin, A. R. *Mining in the East Midlands 1550-1947*. 1971.
Coalmining. Longmans Industrial Archaeology Series, 1971.
The British Coalmining Industry, Retrospect and Prospect. Buxton, 1977.
Hair, T. H. *Sketches of the Coal Mines in Northumberland and Durham*. 1844; reprinted Newton Abbot, 1969.
Lewis, M. J. T. *Early Wooden Railways*. 1970.
Nef, J. U. *The Rise of the British Coal Industry*. 2 volumes, 1932.
Taylor, T. J. *The Archaeology of the Coal Trade*. 1858.